MORE SERMON OUTLINES
ON
PRAYER

Books by Al Bryant

Climbing the Heights
Day by Day with C. H. Spurgeon
More Sermon Outlines for Special Occasions
More Sermon Outlines on Prayer
New Every Morning
Revival Sermon Outlines
Sermon Outlines for Evangelistic Occasions
Sermon Outlines for Funerals and Other Special Occasions
Sermon Outlines for Lay Leaders
Sermon Outlines on Bible Characters (Old Testament)
Sermon Outlines on Bible Characters (New Testament)
Sermon Outlines on the Attributes of God
Sermon Outlines on the Deeper Life
Sermon Outlines on the Cross of Christ
Sermon Outlines on the Life of Christ
Sermon Outlines on Prayer
Sermon Outlines on Prophetic Themes
Sermon Outlines for Special Occasions
Sermon Outlines for Worship Services
Sourcebook of Poetry

MORE SERMON OUTLINES
ON
PRAYER

compiled by
Al Bryant

Grand Rapids, MI 49501

More Sermon Outlines on Prayer by Al Bryant.

Copyright © 1995 by Kregel Publications, a division of Kregel, Inc., P. O. Box 2607, Grand Rapids, MI 49501. Kregel Publications provides trusted, biblical publications for Christian growth and service. Your comments and suggestions are valued.

All rights reserved. No part of this book may be reproduced, stored in a retrieval system, or transmitted in any form or by any means—electronic, mechanical, photocopy, recording, or otherwise—without written permission of the publisher, except for brief quotations in printed reviews.

Cover and Book Design: Alan G. Hartman

Library of Congress Cataloging-in-Publication Data
Bryant, Al
   More sermon outlines on prayer / [compiled by] Al Bryant.
  p. cm.
  1. Prayer—Sermons—Outlines, syllabi, etc.
I. Bryant, Al, 1926–   .
BV213.M   1995   252'.02—dc20   95-6427
                                                                CIP

ISBN 0-8254-2190-x (paperback)

2 3 4 5 Printing / Year 99

Printed in the United States of America

CONTENTS

Preface 7
Scripture Index 8

Part 1: Sermon Outlines on Prayer
The Prayer of Faith 9
How to Pray 9
Humanity's Greatest Prayer 10
The Lord's Prayer 11
Our Daily Bread 12
Asking, Seeking, Knocking 13
Corporate Prayer 14
Into the Woods 15
Why Pray? 17
The Prayer Habits of Jesus 18
A Petition in Prayer 19
The Pattern Prayer 20
Prayer's Power 20
Prayer Examined and Analyzed 21
Militant Prayer 22
"Behold He Prayeth" 23
A Prayer Meeting in Apostolic Times 24
The Christian's Warfare 25
The Power of Prayer 26
Daniel—Man for All Seasons 27
Prevalent Prayer 28
Christ's Wonderful Prayer Promises 29
Twelve Principles of Prayer 30
Seven Samples of Prayer in Luke 31
Why Our Prayers Are Not Answered 31
The Prayer of Faith 32
Prayer 33
Some Conclusions About Prayer 34
Jesus, the Man of Prayer 35

Part 2: Miscellaneous Themes Suitable for Deeper-Life Emphasis

Old Testament
Walking with God 36

Walking with God 36
The Burning Bush an Emblem of the Church 37
How to "Be Strong" 37
A Great God 38
Loyalty to God's House 38
Remember Egypt! 39
The Everlasting Arms 40
Saints in God's Hand 41
Seven-Fold Privilege of the Child of God 42
The Happy People 42
Love for the House of God 43
A Call to Worship 44
Together 45
Follow Your Leader 45
The Eternal City 46
The Purpose of Praise 46
The Merchant 47
Seven Reasons for Studying the Bible 49
The Prayers to Which God Listens 50
Our Wonderful Savior 50
The Threefold Work of the Holy Spirit 51
What Daniel Was 51
The Best Protection 52
With Wings as Eagles 53
The Antidote to Fear 54
Witnesses 55
The Desire of All Nations 56
Spiritual Worship 57

New Testament
The Name of Jesus 58
The Christian's Light 59
The Duty of Disciples 60
Confessing Christ 61
The Easy Yoke and the Light Burden 62
The Believer's Position 62
The Presence of Jesus 63
Great Faith 64

PREFACE

The dictionary offers a concept or definition of the word "concert" we don't often think about: "agreement of two or more individuals in a design or plan; combined action; accord or harmony." A "concerted" effort is then: "contrived or arranged by agreement; planned or devised together; done or performed together or in cooperation." When I think of the corporate aspect of prayer (which is the subject of this compilation), I cannot help but think of our Lord's promise in Matthew 18:20, "Where two or three are gathered, there am I in the midst."

That is the picture of prayer emphasized in this collection. There are sermon outlines on prayer (including several on the Lord's Prayer, our model) and related subjects which we have chosen to call *More Sermon Outlines on Prayer*. The first section offers a score or more outlines dealing specifically with prayer while the second part of the book provides sermon outlines on various subjects suitable for use in services where prayer and the deeper life of faith are encouraged.

One of my favorite poems is entitled *What Is Prayer?* It was penned by James Montgomery, and its first stanza supports what I have been saying:

> Prayer is the soul's sincere desire,
> Uttered or unexpressed;
> The motion of a hidden fire
> That trembles in the breast.

May God add His blessing to these ventures into His Word.

Al Bryant

SCRIPTURE INDEX

Genesis
5:22 36

Ecodus
3:2 37

Deuteronomy
5:15 39
33:3 41
33:3–29 42
33:27 40
33:27–29 42

Joshua
1 37

2 Chronicles
16:9 38

Nehemiah
10:39 38

Psalms
26:8 43
34:3 44
55:14 45
78:53 45
87:3 46
103:2 46
119:11 49

Proverbs
3:14 47
15:29 50

Isaiah
9:6 50
26:3 52
40:31 53
41:10 54
43:10 55

Daniel
6 51
6:3–28 27

Haggai
2:7 56

Matthew
1:21 58
5:16 59
6:5–7 9
6:6–14 9
6:9–13 ..... 10, 11
6:11 12
6:33 60
7:7 13
10:32 61
11:30 62
14:25–33 63

15:28 64
18:20 14

Mark
14:35 15

Luke
11:1 17
11:2 19
11:2–4 20
18:1 21

John
4:23 57
16:7–11 51
17:6 62

Acts
4:31 .... 20, 22
9:11 23
12:5 24

2 Corinthians
10:4 25

Ephesians
3:16 26

James
5:16 28

Part 1: Sermon Outlines on Prayer

THE PRAYER OF FAITH

Matthew 6:6–14

There are many prayers in which God probably sees some good, which cannot claim the abounding promise of the text. It becomes then a question of infinite importance: What are the attributes of that prayer to which this glorious promise is made? Though I know little about it, as far as I am taught, they are the eight following:

1. Earnest Desire
2. Submission
3. Dependence
4. An Earnest and Diligent Use of Means
5. Deep Humility
6. Faith
7. Perseverance
8. An Absorbing Regard for the Glory of God

E. D. Griffin

HOW TO PRAY

Matthew 6:5–7

1. Pray in your own room—secret communion (Matt. 6:6).
2. Give thanks to God—true gratitude (John 11:41; 1 Thess. 5:18).
3. Tell Him of your sins—true confession (Ps. 51).
4. Avoid vain repetitions—true earnestness (Matt. 6:7).
5. Pray in all sincerity—with a true heart (Heb. 10:22).
6. Faint not—pray always (Luke 18:1).
7. Make your life a life of prayer—day and night (1 Tim. 5:5).
8. God loves to hear the prayers of His children (Isa. 65:24).

A. B. Carrero

HUMANITY'S GREATEST PRAYER

Matthew 6:9–13

The Lord's Prayer contains just six petitions divided into two groups of three each. It is significant that the first group begins the prayer. They have to do with the interests of God.

I. The Interests of God

A. "Our Father . . . Hallowed be thy name." We put ourselves and our own interests away as we seek to enter the presence of God.

B. "Thy kingdom come." This is a great broadening petition. Our Lord was speaking of His eternal kingdom.

C. "Thy will be done." This is the way that the kingdom shall come.

God's will for each of us is something fine, constructive, uplifting. No one need fear to pray this prayer as though it involved accepting something dreadful. It is a great ringing cry for God's will to be done here as it is in heaven—and that means happily, triumphantly, gloriously.

II. Our Interests

A. "Give us our daily bread." This word "bread" probably should be expanded to include our basic needs. Yet, as has been pointed out, no man can pray for his daily bread and forget the other fellow. The prayer is for "us," not "me."

B. "Forgive us our debts as we forgive our debtors." What Jesus says in this prayer is, "Forgive others and God will forgive us."

There is a social note here, too.

"We do pray for mercy; and that same prayer doth teach us all to render deeds of mercy" (Shakespeare).

C. "Lead us not into temptation, but deliver us from evil."

The prayer closes with the thought of life as a moral battlefield. The supreme peril is not physical or material; it is moral. People have sometimes stumbled over the wording here. "Would God lead us into temptation?" they ask. The answer is that Hebrew literary form dearly loves the use of parallelism. "Lead us not into temptation" and "deliver us from evil" mean just the same: Prevent us being brought into temptation too great for us to conquer.

Albert W. Palmer

THE LORD'S PRAYER

Matthew 6:9–13

This prayer is not short as would appear. If measured by its contents, it is longer than Solomon's prayer at the dedication of the Temple. Every word is weighty.

"Our Father." Madame de Gasparin said that if Jesus had done nothing on earth but reveal the truth contained in those two words He would have conferred an inestimable blessing on the human race.

The word "our" teaches the oneness of the church.

I. This is not called "The Lord's Prayer" because He Himself had need of it.

II. It was intended as a model: "After this manner therefore pray ye."

A. *It is a model in brevity*—There is no superfluous word. "Ye shall not be heard for your much speaking."

B. *Also in directness*—There is no beating about the bush, but a direct shot to the mark. It is as if Jesus said, "When you pray, ask for what you want; nothing more, nothing less."

C. *And in comprehensiveness*—It is difficult to think of any need which is not included in the six petitions of this prayer. The first three have to do with the divine glory: God's name, His kingdom, His will; fulfilled in the life and character of men. The other three concern the welfare of men: bread, pardon of sin, support in trial and deliverance.

III. Then the ascription: "For Thine is the Kingdom," etc. It is a logical sequence of the foregoing petitions since it declares the divine ability to supply all need.

IV. Amen. This means not merely "so be it," but "so it shall be." It is an avowal of the suppliant's confidence in God, as answerer of prayer.

J. Ellis

A preacher, while watching a marble cutter at work, exclaimed: "I wish I could deal such clanging blows on stony hearts!"

The workman replied: "Maybe you could if you worked like me, on your knees." *Gib McMasters*

OUR DAILY BREAD

Matthew 6:11

One of the reasons why the Lord's Prayer appeals to all of us is that it shows that our Lord really understands our needs. It is . . .

1. A Practical Prayer

Here Jesus recognizes the physical basis of life. Men must have food, and He who said that man could not live by bread alone knew also that man could not live *without* bread. The Master never despised the needs of the body. If others had been giving this prayer, they might have made this the last of our personal requests, but not so with Him.

Many people can see in this prayer that Jesus is interested in a primary economic question. He sees the quest of the ages for bread. He pictures the caravans of the early nations going forth to find pasturage. He sees modern nations seeking a place in the world for their people.

This prayer is a constant reminder that the smallest and most common things in life should be taken to God in prayer. We are not entirely dependent upon our own efforts. God is the Great Supplier.

2. A Simple Prayer

The simplicity of the prayer is seen in its modest request. We live in a time of abundance. We are confused by the plenty.

As Socrates sat meditating with a smile upon his face one day, a friend asked the cause of his satisfaction. He replied that he was just thinking of how many things he could be happy without.

This prayer is simple in asking for bread instead of the luxuries. It is simple in asking for tomorrow's bread rather than in asking for much through the years which are to come. It is a faith-building prayer because it takes into account that God will be with us.

3. An Unselfish Prayer

Its plea is not "give me," but "give *us*."

It gathers in its arms all of the hungry people in the world, the neighbor's hungry children and the famine-stricken child in the third world. It reaches from San Francisco to Shanghai, from Chicago to Calcutta. It unites the things which never should be parted, bread and brotherhood.

Many of us have found the presence of God when we have sought to minister to the needs of others. *Arthur E. Cowley*

ASKING, SEEKING, KNOCKING

Matthew 7:7

One can get anything he wants, if he wants it deeply enough and long enough, if he feels that he will die if he does not get it. How much do you want God? Would you die to have Him? Would you give your life to possess Him? Is He worth living for and dying for? Is He necessary for your happiness? Do you feel that you cannot live without Him? Here is the prayer life. First, a request, then a pursuit, then an assault. How far has choice driven us toward God?

1. A Request

God is accessible. Nothing can block the one who seeks God in prayer. A priest or preacher is not necessary. A prayer book is not essential. It is not necessary to know pious phrases. Anyone, anytime, may have access to God. He is always available. Of course you must ask for the right things. Judgment is necessary. If you ask for something which might hurt you or your family, God should not give it to you. The rich fool made his prayer. He asked for larger barns and greater crops. God let him have them.

2. Pursuit

Persistent prayer is more than an asking. It is a pursuit. One may be so persistent that he pesters God. If the door is closed, he forces his way in and demands a hearing. He may get up from his knees to force his demands. God will not punish him for the effrontery. Indeed, He has given permission for this pursuit. "Seek, and ye shall find."

Here, again, one must be sure that he is seeking for the right thing. Assume that you are to get what you seek. Is it what you need? Would the way take you to Sodom or Zion? What kind of home would it give you? Would it take you to the hills of God or the valley of death?

3. Assault

But God invites this too. He says: "The Kingdom of Heaven suffereth violence, and men of violence take it by force." He seems to challenge us to storm heaven.

But be sure that it is the door of God's house at which you knock. Suppose that God should give you what you so violently demand. What effect would it have on you?

James I. Vance

CORPORATE PRAYER

Matthew 18:20

The point for us to consider here is how the fellowship mentioned in our text is achieved. It is where two or three are "gathered together," "in my name," that Jesus Christ is specially manifest. They must be together, soul in soul, and they must be together in His name—that is, in the character of Christ, reaching up to His purity, to His prayer.

I. Belief in Corporate Prayer

Jesus had a right to expect that corporate judgment would reach a purity of morality and character superior to that of the individual. We do not gain from this any idea of the infallibility of the Church. We do, however, deduct a general principle that in the majority of instances it is a distinct gain for Christians to pray together rather than separately. Where there is a group thus engaged in prayer, the presence of Christ will come more fully than is possible to the individual who is praying alone.

A. One hindrance to the presence of Christ in a service is the presence of those who have no interest in the prayer. They come in alone, they remain alone, they depart alone. They neither worship nor pray.

B. What is most needed today is a mass morality commensurate with the sterling individual morality of a generation ago. Perhaps this can best be grown through corporate prayer.

II. Method

Much of the impatience with prayer may be traced to the lack of preparation which was thought to be honoring the Holy Spirit. The result was often a wearisome repetition of the same petitions and a clumsiness and slovenliness of feeble utterance. The time has come for laymen as well as preachers to take this matter seriously.

A. One effective method is the silent, guided prayer. The leader states simply the theme of intercession. Then the congregation is asked to present their own silent petitions to the throne of God. There are two advantages to this. One is that with many different petitions all phases of the theme will doubtless be covered. The second is that the silence provides a spiritual unity.

B. Everything depends upon the devotional spirit of the meeting. There must be a serene and devotional spirit between the prayers, not merely an anxious and impatient longing that someone will pick up the prayer. No one should take part merely for the sake of doing so.

C. Experience reveals that small groups are more effective than large groups for these spiritual experiences. As numbers increase, we run the risk of impurity of thought. On the other hand, great meetings offer a tremendous opportunity for education in prayer and prayer methods.

If we could secure in the Christian church throughout the world the mass praying of Mohammedanism while making such prayer really Christian, we should take the kingdom of God by storm.

Albert D. Belden

INTO THE WOODS

Mark 14:35

In a little English village there is a cenotaph which bears this inscription: "Aye, aye, sir, and farther." It is in honor of a World War I soldier. When he had been asked if he would go where duty required, he answered: "Aye, aye, sir, and farther."

The three disciples went a little farther into the Garden than the other eight. They went with Jesus under the trees. They slept, but He went still farther.

1. Prayer

It is recorded of Jesus that He worked, ate, slept, wept, walked, rode, and about twenty-five times, that He prayed. No doubt He was taught to pray by His mother when as a child He knelt by His little bed. He prayed when He toiled as a carpenter and when He went into the synagogue on the Sabbath days. He prayed when He fed the five thousand; before the tomb of Lazarus, and when He went out alone; but by far His most important prayer was this short one He expressed in the Garden that night.

Many people only pray when they want something. When they are sick, they pray for health; when they are in danger, they pray for safety; during a drought, they pray for rain. There is another kind of praying which seeks to change the will of God. But that is not the prayer of Jesus.

"All prayer is to change the human will into submission to the divine will" (F. W. Robertson). C. S. Lewis says, "Prayer does not change God. It changes *me*."

That was the purport of the prayer of Jesus in the Garden. "Not My will, but Thine."

2. Service

Jesus found out as He went a little farther that if He was to serve, He must suffer. Of course He had partially discovered this before. But now He faced the greatest cost.

The story is told of two little lakes. Both stood amid the hills. One decided to stand and enjoy itself. It gradually dried up. The other broke through the mountains and trickled down until it came to a stream. It joined this and went on until it came to a river. Then it went on out into the ocean. Finally one day the lake which the water had left was surprised to see it coming back from the clouds. That is the way of life. Returns come through giving.

There are two bodies of water in the Holy Land about which this is eminently true—the Dead Sea and the Sea of Galilee. The first is stagnant, dead, and stinking because it has no outlet. The second is vibrantly healthy and alive because it flows out, giving away its bounty.

3. Strengthened

Jesus went a little farther than the three, and He was met by a messenger of God.

Who are they who see visions and hear voices? Those who go out, a little farther. Abraham became the friend of God because he went out not knowing whither he went. Moses saw a bush that burned and was not consumed because he went out a little farther. Paul saw the man from Macedonia and heard his cry because he went out farther than any other messenger of Christ.

The eight who slept by the gate merely had a night's rest. The three who woke and dosed merely rested. The Master went a little farther.

A. R. Johns

WHY PRAY?

Luke 11:1

The Malay tribes, before going to hunt elephants, have a form of prayer offered to their idols which leads them to anoint their bodies with four kinds of aromatic ointment which serve in fact to deaden their bodies, so there is no pain from injury to the hunter, and thus they are more successful. Other heathen tribes dance in a ritual of religious worship and by the dance work up their courage and then give their god credit for the ability to go out and fight fearlessly. How like the Pharisees are these systems. Instead of lifting men they burden them.

1. Prayer Lifts

"Many times I have been driven to my knees when I had no place else to go" (Abraham Lincoln).

"I fear John Knox's prayers more than I do ten thousand soldiers" (Mary Queen of Scots).

Hornaday points out that there are three Greek words for prayer. First, *homage*; second, *communication*; and, third, *supplication*. St. Theresa says that there are three requisites for successful prayer. First, *love for one another*; second, *disengagement from every affection of a creature or material kind*; third, *humility*.

2. Prayer Develops the Spiritual Nature

Prayer develops the spiritual nature as music does the aesthetic. It enthrones the eternal which is in man. Then man begins to see God more clearly. He understands when the answers to prayer are delayed. Long before Augustine caught a vision of God, Monica, his mother, had been wrestling in prayer.

At Torthawald a dissolute woman used to crowd to the window to listen to John G. Paton as he conducted family prayers. She felt that when he prayed, "Convert the sinner from the error of his way," that he meant her. The burden was placed on her heart, and she was converted. The prayer of a devout man had built the spiritual life in her. Praying for others not only helps the person for whom we pray, but it helps ourselves.

3. Prayer Needs Its Quiet Times

We can pray effectively only when we are alone with God. Jesus Himself went apart in the mountains. Jacob did not know the exact title of the One with whom he wrestled; prosperity and fear had blurred his vision, but his earnest persistency found a way through the darkness, and he knew in "whom he believed." The doubter who honestly seeks God in quiet and with sincere thoughtfulness will hear His voice and find the "way."

4. Prayer Must Include Confession

The angel asked Jacob his identity. When he gave it, he confessed his sinfulness. Then he could cry, "God be merciful to me a sinner." In prayer we are coming to the Great Physician. Before we can be helped, we must admit our weakness. Formal petitions are not necessary, but we must put ourselves in our prayers.

C. F. Reisner

THE PRAYER HABITS OF JESUS

I. How He Prayed
A. Usually alone (Matt. 14:23; Luke 5:16; 9:18; 22:41).
B. With others (Luke 9:28; 10:21; 11:1).

II. When He Prayed
A. In the early morning (Mark 1:35).
B. All night (Luke 6:12).
C. In great crises:
  1. At His baptism (Luke 3:21).
  2. At the raising of Lazarus (John 11:41–42).
  3. In the Garden (Matt. 26:39, 42, 44).
  4. On the Cross (Matt. 27:46).

III. Where He Prayed

We learn from the records that He prayed most often at a great distance from everyone, choosing nearly always a quiet spot. His favorite places of prayer were the hilltops back of Nazareth, the slopes of Olivet, and the hillsides overlooking the Lake of Galilee.

E. P. Lananan

To neglect prayer is to burden ourselves with care, to shut ourselves out of blessing, to enfeeble our faith, to dim the eyes of our hope, to dampen the fire of our zeal, to relax the grip of our tenacity, to weaken the heart of love, and to rob ourselves of its strength.

F. E. Marsh

A PETITION IN PRAYER

Thy will be done, as in heaven, so in earth (Luke 11:2).

The chief meaning of this petition is not that we should suffer, but that we should act. With earnest and firm resolve we should set ourselves upon doing that which our own consciences tell us God would have us to do. But let us consider, first, its bearing upon suffering.

I. **Though This Is a Part of the Meaning of the Petition, It Is but a Small Part.**

A. God has so formed the world that trouble is part of our common lot, falling upon some but lightly and at distant intervals, and visiting others blow upon blow until their hearts are bowed down and overclouded with sorrow.

B. Our reason tells us that to submit to God's law is wise. But when our own turn comes to suffer, our will rises against God, and it is faith only that can make us say, "Thy will be done"—faith in God's love, in Christ's salvation, and in the promised glory of Christ's kingdom.

II. **The More Important Meaning of the Petition Is "Thy Will Be Done" Actively by Us, by Our Earnestly Setting Ourselves to Live a Life of Faith.**

A. This is the more important for two reasons:
1. Because it is the true meaning of the petition, not "Thy will be endured," but "Thy will be done."
2. It is to be done as in heaven.
3. But there is no suffering in heaven.
4. Besides, the doing of God's will includes the bearing of it as the cause includes the effect.
5. All we can do is by the grace of God. To obtain this grace we must pray.

III. **God's Will Must Not Only Be Done, but Done As His Will.**

A. How this is to be is to be seen by our Lord's example.

B. That is the hardest thing of all—to do God's will.
1. We can because our natures have been transformed, all selfishness and earthly longing removed, and the image of God once again restored in our defiled and sin-corrupted breasts.

Three Hundred Outlines on the New Testament

THE PATTERN PRAYER

Luke 11:2–4

A child's prayer—Our Father. He pities us in all sorrow and sin. Gives us all we need.

A saint's prayer—Hallow, reverence. Love first and then reverence.

A subject's prayer—Kingdom of God to be widened by us in spreading the knowledge of His love.

A servant's prayer—Not think God's will hard, difficult, or painful. Submit to it joyfully.

A dependent's prayer—We like to be independent, but it is a mistake. Bread is God's good gift. We plow the fields and scatter, etc. He sends the rain.

A sinner's prayer—Put things right by God's help. We pray for mercy, but let us do deeds of mercy.

A traveler's prayer—From evil. Boys like adventure. Watch and pray, lest we enter into temptation.   *Author Unknown*

PRAYER'S POWER

Acts 4:31

1. Prayer Has a Separation Power—The cleansing of the temple and Nehemiah's prayer (Neh. 1:5–11).
2. Prayer Has a Saving Power—"Lord, save me" (Matt. 14:30).
3. Prayer Has a Solacing Power—Sorrow filled the hearts of John's disciples after he was beheaded, but they were comforted after they had told Jesus (Matt. 14:12).
4. Prayer Has a Strengthening Power—Heaven's angel strengthened Jesus in the Garden.
5. Prayer Has a Spoiling Power—Jehoshaphat prayed and the Lord spoiled the Moabites and Ammonites (2 Chron. 20:6–12, 25).
6. Prayer Has a Staying Power—Paul, because he was a praying warrior, was an ardent worker. In 1 Thessalonians 2:9, he says "night and day."
7. Prayer Has a Stirring Power—It stirs us out of lethargy and laziness. When there is a lack of prayer, then there will be an absence of power.

Author Unknown

PRAYER EXAMINED AND ANALYZED

Luke 18:1

I. **The Nature of Prayer**

Prayer is the presentation of our heart's desires to God, entreating Him to regard them according to His gracious will. Formally it may be regarded as including Adoration or Reverence, Confession, Petition, and Thanksgiving. Prayer includes—

A. A *knowledge of God.* As the God of grace through Christ. As a sin-forgiving God—an all-sufficient God—as bountiful and compassionate—as omnipresent, omniscient, and omnipotent—as the Father of Christ, and our Father in Him.

B. A *knowledge of ourselves.* As sinners—as ignorant, weak, impure, as heirs of immortality. As having great duties to perform—malignant foes to encounter—as having to honor God.

C. *Faith in Christ* as the medium of access to God—faith in His intercession (John 14:13–14; Heb. 4:15–16).

D. *The assistance of the Holy Spirit* (Rom. 8:26).

E. Petition for blessings *suitable to God's will* (1 John 5:14).

F. *Sincerity* (Ps. 66:18).

G. *Fervency.* Not the energy and warmth of the animal spirits, but the inward feeling of the heart expressed in prayer (James 5:6).

II. **The Constancy of Prayer**

"People ought always," etc.

There is a disposition to *faint.* From the pressure of worldly cares—from prayer not being immediately answered—from fear of man on public occasions—from spiritual declension, neglect of prayer being one of the first signs of that declension—*where the heart is not engaged, prayer will soon become a burden.*

But everyone ought *always* to pray. When the appointments of the church call—when spiritual conflicts alarm—when important duties are to be discharged.

We shall always be surrounded with sin; the enemy of souls will never cease opposition; we shall never be free from wants, never be independent; we are always liable to err and stumble and fall into misery: therefore *people* ought always to pray.

Pray in the closet—in the household—in the temple, and always mentally as the case may require.

If we do not pray, we shall not overcome—not win—not obtain the crown of life. If we do not pray, we shall be lost.

In conclusion, prayer is the very essence of spiritual pleasure and the precursor of everlasting praise.

Those who pray not are ignorant, unsaved, and liable to perish.

102 Sketches and Skeletons

MILITANT PRAYER

Acts 4:31

Introduction

The word "militant" comes from the same root as "militia." A militia is an organized military force which is available for a special service. The Christian is a part of a select group of prayer warriors defending the church of God.

I. The Call to Arms

A. God is searching for consecrated volunteers to save the world (Ezek. 22:30).

B. Now is the time to join in the battle for souls (John 4:35).

II. The Silent Reserve

A. There is a sob in the heart of God because of lack of prayer warriors (Ezek. 22:30; Isa. 59:16).

B. We must exercise our prayer potential. Silent reserves are idlers in the kingdom.

III. The Warrior's Triumph

A. God will aid the crusading soul (Luke 18:7–8).

B. There is power in prevailing prayer (cf. Elijah, Moses).

C. Text says that prayer "shakes" things.

D. There is triumph here and hereafter for God's militiamen.

Raymond C. Kratzer

"BEHOLD HE PRAYETH"

And the Lord said unto him, Arise, and go into the street which is called Straight, and inquire in the house of Judas for one called Saul, of Tarsus: for, behold, he prayeth (Acts 9:11).

I. What Is Prayer?
A. Hebrew word signifying appeal or intercession.
B. The approach on the part of the soul to God in the name of Jesus Christ (John 16:23–24).
C. May consist in invocation, adoration, confession, petition, pleading, dedication, thanksgiving, blessings.
D. Most natural act of a newborn child of God.

II. What Is the Effect of Prayer?
A. It demands our best and brings all that is best to the front.
B. It brings the heart into communion with God.
C. It brings one into conformity to God's will.
D. It brings one into actual dealing with God.

III. What Is the Christian's Attitude Regarding Prayer?
A. It is his vital breath.
B. It is his constant attitude.
C. It is his health, his joy, his life.
D. It is his mightiest weapon, his shield, his victory.
E. It is his lever to move, overthrow, accomplish whatever his faith aspires to according to God's will.

IV. What Has Prayer Accomplished?
A. It culminated in the filling of the Spirit for Paul (v. 17).
B. Our Savior a Man of prayer preeminently.
C. Church born in atmosphere of prayer.
D. Honor roll of Hebrews 11—all people of prayer.
E. Prayer enabled the martyrs to endure.
F. Church of God saved from failure and defeat by prayer.
G. Prayer, pardon, peace, power, purity, paradise.

James F. Spink

A PRAYER MEETING IN APOSTOLIC TIMES

(Acts 12:5)

Peter had continued in prayer for the church, and now the church continues in prayer for him. There is blessed cooperation in the mystical body. It is a proof we are members of this body, if we bear one another's sorrows. Not pity or mere condolence or promise only, but really put our shoulder to the burden.

1. **Observe, in This Case They Confined Their Efforts to Prayer**

   Sometimes we find ourselves in such a position that we can do nothing but pray. Like Israel at the Red Sea: no power of theirs can make a passage through the waters or defeat the oncoming legions; they can only wait on God. Or like Daniel in the lions' den, or Elijah when the rain was withheld. For such times we have a promise, "Ask, and ye shall receive."

2. **Observe, They Continued in This Effort**

   It was no formal or heartless prayer meeting. They must have possessed strong faith. The case seemed hopeless. Tomorrow is fixed for Peter's death (v. 6). The hate of Herod is known to be malignant. James the apostle had been already slain.

3. **They Reaped the Benefit**

   The answer filled them with amazement.

   The answer was superabundant.

   Perhaps they had not prayed for his deliverance that night, or for his deliverance at all, but that he might glorify God in the fire.

   The answer was speedy.

   Stems and Twigs

Heating Apparatus

C. H. Spurgeon was showing some visitors over the Tabernacle (London). After taking them to the main part of the building, he said, "Come, and I'll show you the heating apparatus." Imagine their surprise, when he took them to a room where four hundred were gathered in a prayer meeting. The church with warmth of spirit must have the warmth-producing prayer meeting.

THE CHRISTIAN'S WARFARE

2 Corinthians 10:4

It is a common thing for the apostle to speak of the Christian's life and trials as a warfare (2 Tim. 2:3; 1 Tim. 1:18; Eph. 6:12).

I. The Nature of This Warfare

A. It is a warfare with the corrupt desires and sensual propensities of our fallen nature (Gal. 5:17; 1 Peter 2:11).

B. It is a warfare with the mighty spirits of evil (1 Peter 5:8; Mark 5:9; 2 Cor. 2:11; 11:14).

C. It is a warfare with sin and wickedness in all its forms. Idolatry, infidelity, free-loveism, Cults, licentiousness, intemperance, Sabbath desecration, dishonesty, profaneness and corruptness, in whatever form it may exist.

II. The Enemy's Strongholds

A. *Ignorance—intellectual and spiritual blindness* (Eph. 4:18). Atheists and infidels are ignorant of the Scriptures (Mark 12:24). History shows that ignorance is one of the main pillars of Catholicism. If people only *knew* the evil connected with and resulting from the liquor traffic, they would not tolerate it another year.

B. *Pride.* The very essence of sin is pride—self-exaltation. It has ruined many great and good men. One of the most difficult things to conquer. Man is too proud to confess his sins and his Savior; too proud to stoop down and take hold of and lift up the fallen.

C. *Prejudice.* It blinds the eye and warps the understanding.

D. *Unbelief.* It was unbelief that led the children of Israel so frequently into idolatry (Matt. 13:59).

III. The Weapons of Our Warfare

A. *Negatively.* "Not carnal." Carnal weapons are wealth, fame, worldly power, sword, etc. Mahomet propagated his religion with the sword. Others want to conquer by means of their wealth, social standing, trickery, hypocrisy, violence, etc.

B. *Positively.* The truth (2 Cor. 6:6). The truth of the Gospel is from God; it is permeated by God's spirit and backed by God's power. Thus Christ conquered temptation, Peter won three thousand on Pentecost, etc.

C. *The place of prayer in this battle.*

Author Unknown

THE POWER OF PRAYER

Ephesians 3:16

Introduction
   A. Paul's prayers are impressive and expressive.
   B. This particular prayer is:

I. Expressive of Man's Search for Power
   A. In every sphere of life there is a craving for strength and power.
      1. Physical culturists denounce the crime of being weak.
      2. Current literature tells how to develop mind.
      3. Modern "cultism" seeks "spirit" development.
   B. In "Sesame and Lillies" Ruskin said, "Deep-rooted in human nature there is an inextinguishable love of Power."

II. Expressive of Man's Stronghold of Power
   This strengthening is to be in the inward man.
   A. Man's outer accumulations succumb to life's calamities.
   B. Man's inner achievements survive life's tragedies.

III. Expressive of Man's Source of Power
   A. In ancient literature man is the source of power.
   B. In biblical literature God is the source of power.
   C. The Holy Spirit gives power for all of life.

Conclusion
   Christians need not be weak spiritually.

E. S. Phillips

Prayer Work

"I am sorry I am late today," said a clergyman visiting an aged parishioner, "but I have been all around the parish."

"Why," said the old woman, "that's just where I've been!"

"But you cannot walk!" exclaimed the astonished minister.

"Ah," said the old saint, "you see, my *soul* isn't bedridden! So I just go round the parish every day in prayer, while I lie here."

Weapons for Workers

DANIEL—MAN FOR ALL SEASONS

Daniel 6:3–28

1. **A Praying Man**
   "He kneeled and prayed" (v. 10).
2. **A Praising Man**
   "And gave thanks" (v. 10).
3. **A Persecuted Man**
   "Cast him into the den of lions" (v. 16).
4. **A Protected Man**
   "Hath shut the lions' mouths" (v. 22).
5. **A Persistent Man**
   "Thou servest continually" (v. 20).
6. **A Privileged Man**
   "God, whom thou servest" (v. 20).
7. **A Prosperous Man**
   "So this Daniel prospered" (v. 28).
8. **A Preferred Man**
   "This Daniel was preferred" (v. 3).

Author Unknown

Do I Really Pray?

I often say my prayers,
   But do I really pray?
And do the wishes of my heart
   Go with the words I say?

I may as well kneel down
   And worship gods of stone,
As offer to the living God
   A prayer of words alone.

For words without the heart
   The Lord will never hear;
Nor will He to those lips attend
   Whose prayer is not sincere!

Lord, show me what I need
   And teach me how to pray,
And help me when I seek Thy grace
   To mean the words I say.

John Burton

PREVALENT PRAYER

James 5:16

There is probably nothing connected with practical religion, in regard to which there has been more of superstition on the one hand and of skepticism on the other, than prayer. The tendency of the human mind to rest in that which is formal and visible and to stop short of that which is internal and essential is shown when men, forgetting that God is a Spirit and must be worshiped in spirit and in truth, expect to win His favor by bodily kneelings and verbal utterance of forms of prayer without regard to the condition of their souls.

Some of the most important points in the Bible theory of prayer are:

1. The Character of Those Supposed to Offer the Prayer.

Prayer, to have any influence or efficacy with God, must be the offering of a righteous person.

2. The Character of the Prayer Itself.

It is "effectual fervent prayer." When we hear a man pray, if his words are fit and his manner earnest, we presume that his heart is sincere. Not so with God. The words, the manner, the look and tones are nothing to Him. He sees the heart and has immediate observation of the spirit. Prayer, in order to avail, must not merely *seem*, it must *be*, earnest.

3. Its Efficiency.

The declaration of the text is that it "availeth much." Thus invited and thus assured, can we not carry our petitions to Him, expecting to prevail? *Nelson*

Upon one of D. L. Moody's journeys across the Atlantic there was a fire in the hold of the ship. The crew and some volunteers stood in line to pass buckets of water.

A friend said to Moody, "Mr. Moody, let us go to the other end of the ship and engage in prayer."

The evangelist, with common sense, replied, "Not so, sir; we will stand right here and pass buckets and pray hard all the time we are doing so."

How like Moody this was! He believed that prayer and work were like the two hands of the one person in that they should never be separated. *Watchman Examiner*

CHRIST'S WONDERFUL PRAYER PROMISES

I. **Who Can Pray So God Will Hear?**
   A. Those who believe on Jesus' name (1 John 5:13–15).
   B. The righteous (Ps. 34:15–17; Prov. 15:8, 29).
   C. Those who keep His commandments and do those things pleasing in His sight (1 John 3:22).
   D. Those who abide in Christ (John 15:7).
   E. He who delights himself in God (Ps. 37:4).
   F. He who commits his way unto the Lord (Ps. 37:5).

II. **Promises for Those Who Pray:**
   A. "... as touching anything they shall ask" (Matt. 18:19–20).
   B. "What things soever ye desire..." (Mark 11:24).
   C. "Whatsoever ye ask in my name..." (John 14:13–14).
   D. "Whatsoever ye shall ask the Father..." (John 16:23).
   E. Prayers must be definite, thus: "What wilt thou that I shall do unto you?... Lord, that I may receive my sight" (Mark 10:51).
   F. We should pray believing (Matt. 21:22).

III. **Why Prayers Are Not Answered:**
   A. If I regard iniquity in my heart (Ps. 66:18).
   B. When sin separates us from God (Isa. 59:1–2).
   C. When we have an idol in the heart—anything which we prefer to God (Ezek. 14:3).
   D. When we do not forgive others (Mark 11:25–26).
   E. When we doubt (James 1:5–7, R.V.).

Author Unknown

No Time

An old Indian teacher met a young convert and asked him if he said his prayers regularly.

He answered, "I am a Christian, but I have no time to pray."

"Then you have no time to breathe," said the teacher.

"Oh, I have to make time for that, so as to live."

"Then," said the teacher, "it is just as important to pray as to breathe."

Sunday Circle

TWELVE PRINCIPLES OF PRAYER

The Bible clearly teaches that certain conditions must prevail if we are to be consistent and successful in our prayer lives. Among these are:

> **Faith (James 1:6–8).**
>
> **Meditation (John 14:6).**
>
> **Conciliation (Matt. 5:24; 6:12).**
>
> **Confession (1 John 1:9).**
>
> **Repentance (Ps. 66:18).**
>
> **Assurance (1 John 5:14–15).**
>
> **Submission (Mark 13:36).**
>
> **Obedience (John 9:31).**
>
> **Abiding (John 15:7).**
>
> **Steadfastness (James 1:6).**
>
> **Persistence (Luke 18:1).**
>
> **Patience (Gal. 6:9).**

Are these attitudes evident in my life as I communicate with my heavenly Father? This is the question I must answer if my prayer life is to be effective and meaningful.

J. H. Sammia

Look to the Sky

"We were crawling together through the darkness in an advanced position in the front line trenches. My friend whispered to me that we were approaching an outpost, but I couldn't distinguish it in the darkness of the night. In helping me locate it, he said, 'Lieutentant, the best way to see in the dark is to get close to the ground and look up against the sky.'"

Good advice for the dark days of life: "Get close to the ground" and look up in prayer.

SEVEN SAMPLES OF PRAYER IN LUKE

1. The Pharisee's (17:11–12).
2. The Publican's (18:13).
3. The Penitent's (23:42).
4. The Poor-Rich Man's (16:24).
5. The Professor's (13:25–26).
6. The Pig-feeder's (8:37).
7. A Possessor's (8:38).

Hy Pickering

WHY OUR PRAYERS ARE NOT ANSWERED

As a Christian I need to look at my life honestly and openly to see if I am guilty of allowing any of the following impediments to prayer to enter my life:

1. **Sin (Isa. 59:1–2; Prov. 15:29).**
2. **Regarding iniquity in my heart (Ps. 66:18).**
3. **Not doing that which is pleasing in His sight (1 John 3:22).**
4. **Idol in the heart (Ezek. 14:3).**
5. **Failing to return thanks (Phil. 4:6–7).**
6. **Selfishness (Prov. 21:13).**
7. **Unforgiving spirit (Mark 11:25).**
8. **Wrong motive for asking (James 4:3).**

O Lord, I pray that none of these attitudes will find room in my life. Keep me from failing to give you free reign in my heart. Amen.

A. T. Pierson

THE PRAYER OF FAITH

The prayer of faith, like some plant rooted in a fruitful soil, draws its virtue from a disposition that has been brought into conformity with the mind of Christ.

1. It is subject to the divine will—"This is the assurance we have in approaching God: that if we ask anything according to his will, he hears us" (1 John 5:14).

2. It is restrained within the interest of Christ—"And I will do whatever you ask in my name, so that the Son may bring glory to the Father" (John 14:13).

3. It is instructed in the truth—"If you remain in me and my words remain in you, ask whatever you wish, and it will be given you" (John 15:7).

4. It is energized by the Spirit—"Now to him who is able to do immeasurably more than all we ask or imagine, according to his power that is at work within us" (Eph. 3:20).

5. It is interwoven with love and mercy—"And when you stand praying, if you hold anything against anyone, forgive him, so that your Father in heaven may forgive you your sins" (Mark 11:25).

6. It is accompanied with obedience—"We have confidence before God and receive from him anything we ask, because we obey his commands and do what pleases him" (1 John 3:21–22).

7. It is so earnest that it will not accept denial—"Ask and it will be given to you; seek and you will find; knock and the door will be opened to you" (Luke 11:9).

8. It goes out to look for and to hasten its answer—"The prayer of a righteous man is powerful and effective" (James 5:16).

Sibbes wrote that "in prayer we tempt God if we ask for that which we labor not. Our faithful endeavors must second our devotion.... If we pray for grace and neglect the spring from which it comes, how can we succeed? It was a rule in ancient times that said, 'Lay thy hand to the plow, and then pray.' No man should pray without plowing, nor plow without prayer."

David M'Intyre

PRAYER

Opening hymn: "What a Friend We Have in Jesus"

I. **Opening Thoughts on Prayer**
   A. Our model (Matt. 6:9–13).
   B. Prayer commanded (Isa. 55:6; Matt. 7:7; Phil. 4:6).

II. **To Be Offered:**
   A. Through Christ (Eph. 2:18; Heb. 10:19).
   B. In faith (Heb. 10:22).
   C. In full assurance of faith (Heb. 11:6).
   D. With confidence in God (John 5:14).
   E. With boldness (Heb. 4:16).
   F. In watchfulness (Luke 21:36).
   G. With obedience (John 9:31).

III. **Some Further Thoughts on Prayer**
   A. Shortness of time a motive (1 Peter 4:7).
   B. Christ present (Matt. 18:20).
   C. God's willingness to give (Matt. 7:11).
   D. Paul and Silas (Acts 16:25).
   E. Without ceasing (1 Thess. 5:17).

Closing hymn: "Prayer Is the Soul's Sincere Desire"

W. H. Grimes

Someone asked Emily Post, "What is the correct procedure when one is invited to the White House and has a previous engagement?" She answered, "An invitation to lunch or dine at the White House is a command, and automatically cancels any other engagement." The Christian should have a daily engagement—with priority claim over everything—to meet the Lord in the secret place of prayer. *Good News Broadcaster*

SOME CONCLUSIONS ABOUT PRAYER

1. **Remember whatever we pray for should interest and deeply concern us.**
   Examples:
   OT: Gen. 32:9–12, 24, 26; 1 Sam. 1:10; Dan. 2:17, 9:17–20
   NT: Matt. 15:22, 25; Luke 8:24, 41; Matt. 26:38.

2. **We must feel that of ourselves we are utterly unable to accomplish what we want.**
   Examples:
   OT: Ps. 124:2; Dan. 2:18
   NT: Matt. 8:24; John 15:5.

3. **We must feel that God is interested and concerned in what interests and concerns us.**
   Examples:
   OT: Gen. 21:12–20; Ps. 146:7–9, 147:9
   NT: Matt. 6:28; 1 Tim. 2:3–4; 1 Peter 5:6–7.

4. **We must feel that God is able to do all we ask of Him.**
   Examples:
   OT: Jer. 32:17–18
   NT: Mark 9:19; Matt. 19:26.

5. **We must feel that God is *accessible* or *open to receive us*.**

J. C. Douglas

Michelangelo once called upon his young pupil Raphael. The latter was not in his studio, but there was a cramped, meager design of his on the canvas. Michelangelo drew with a piece of chalk underneath the poor sketch a bold, sweeping line, and added the word, *Amplius*. When Raphael came in he took the hint, changed his style, and became one of the first of immortal painters. Is not this the trouble with our prayers? They are cramped, meager, narrow, selfish, revolving largely around ourselves and our immediate relatives and friends. Would not the Master write over them, *Amplius*! *Amplius*! Wider and wider! Broader and broader! Deeper and deeper! More and more!

Selected

JESUS, THE MAN OF PRAYER

A look at the earthly life of Jesus offers us a panoramic view of what prayer can mean in the life of a Christian. Jesus prayed:

1. **At His baptism: while He was praying the Holy Spirit came upon Him (Luke 3:21–22).**
2. **He prayed after He had healed many sick (Mark 1:35).**
3. **When His fame spread and multitudes came to hear (Luke 5:16).**
4. **When enemies sought to destroy Him and before appointing disciples (Luke 6:2–12).**
5. **When He had fed five thousand (Mark 14:21–23).**
6. **When praying alone, told His disciples He must be rejected and slain (Luke 9:18).**
7. **When He was transfigured (Luke 9:28).**
8. **At the grave of Lazarus (John 11:41).**
9. **When He taught His disciples to pray (Luke 11:1).**
10. **When His soul was troubled (John 12:27).**
11. **When about to leave His disciples in a world of tribulation (John 17).**
12. **In the Garden of Gethsemane (Matt. 26:36).**
13. **For those who crucified Him (Luke 23:34).**
14. **Jesus resigned His life in prayer (Luke 23:46).**

Thus we see that prayer permeated His life on earth from beginning to end. Should it mean less to us His followers?

Author Unknown

Part 2: Miscellaneous Themes Suitable for Deeper-Life Emphasis
Old Testament

WALKING WITH GOD

Enoch walked with God (Gen. 5:22).

We read of walking before, after, and with God. In the first we have the thought of perfection (Gen. 17:11). In the second, obedience (Deut. 13:4). But in the third, of friendship and fellowship (Gen. 5:25).

I. God Wants Us to Walk with Him (1 Cor. 1:9)
   A. John 1:3; Matthew 11:28. The yoke suggests two who are united.

II. Conditions
   A. Acquaintance (Job 22:21).
   B. Agreement (Amos 3:3).

III. How Are We to Walk?
   A. By Faith (2 Cor. 5:7).
   B. In the Light (1 John 1:7).
   C. In the Newness of Life (Rom. 6:4).
   D. In the Spirit (Gal. 5:16).
   E. In Love (Eph. 5:1–2).
   F. Circumspectly (Eph. 5:15–16).
   G. Worthily (Eph. 4:1).

Sermon Starters, P. E. Holdcraft

WALKING WITH GOD

And Enoch walked with God (Gen. 5:22).

1. **Implies Fellowship with God.**
2. **Implies Service for God.**
3. **Implies Progress in Holy Living.**
4. **Brings Assurance of Safety.**
5. **Gets You Somewhere.** *Sermon Starters*, P. E. Holdcraft

THE BURNING BUSH AN EMBLEM OF THE CHURCH

And the angel of the LORD appeared unto him in a flame of fire out of the midst of a bush: and he looked, and, behold, the bush burned with fire, and the bush was not consumed (Ex. 3:2).

I. **The True Church of God Is Not Associated with Earthly Grandeur and Magnificence.**

II. **The Condition of the Church Has Ever Been That of Trial and Suffering.**

III. **The Church of God Has Within It the Element of Perpetuity.** "Not Burn"—Not Consumed.
   A. Look at this as a striking fact.
   B. For this there is a sufficient reason—God was in the bush. Therefore
      1. Understand the nature of Christ's church.
      2. Abhor persecution.
      3. Look to God our Father for success.
      4. Sympathize with the persecuted and the tried.

The Tool Basket

HOW TO "BE STRONG"

As illustrated in the exhortation to Joshua (Josh. 1)

1. **God's Promise** to rest on—"Be strong, for thou shalt cause this people to inherit" (v. 6)

2. **God's Precepts** to rejoice in—"Be strong and very courageous, that thou mayest observe to do" (v. 7)

3. **God's Presence** to realize daily—"Be strong and of good courage, for the Lord thy God is with thee" (v. 9)

4. **God's People** to be responsible for—"Only be strong and of a good courage" (v. 18)

Twelve Baskets Full

A GREAT GOD

2 Chronicles 16:9

1. **He Sees**—"The eyes of the Lord."
2. **He Acts**—"run to and fro."
3. **He Is Interested**—"throughout the whole earth."
4. **He Manifests Himself**—"to show himself strong."
5. **He Helps**—"in behalf of them."
6. **He Encourages**—"Whose heart is perfect toward him."

Snappy Sermon Starters

LOYALTY TO GOD'S HOUSE

We will not forsake the house of our God (Neh. 10:39).

1. **Because it is the place where God dwells.**
2. **Because it is the place where He reveals Himself.**
3. **Because it is the place where He teaches.**
4. **Because it is the place where He converts.**
5. **Because it is the place where He sanctifies.**
6. **Because it is the place where He hears prayer.**
7. **Because it is the place where He prepares the saints for heaven.**

Snappy Sermon Starters

Faith Forward

A gentleman wanted to try a new shower bath. He turned a tap which he thought would produce a shower of water. Nothing happened. He tried repeatedly and then gave up in despair. Before next morning he made inquiries and found that, in addition to turning the tap, *he should have immediately stepped forward* onto the board immediately under the spray which released a spring. It is not enough to pray; we must step forward in faith.

Selected

REMEMBER EGYPT!

. . . remember that thou wast a servant in the land of Egypt (Deut. 5:15).

We are prone to remember the palaces and pleasures of Egypt. God admonishes us to remember its slavery. The memory of our former state should be:

1. An Antidote to Discontent

Though the labors and trials of the wilderness are many, yet in Egypt we had more.

If we labor, it is not to make bricks without straw. If we are bereaved, at least we can bury our dead. Formerly our toil was for another, now it redounds to our own profit.

2. A Stimulus to Zeal

Remembering Egypt, let us press on toward Canaan; let us give no advantage to our enemies. Knowing the terror of former slavery, fight bravely, that none may reduce us again to that condition.

3. A Reason for Obedience

Surely He who was so gracious as to deliver us has a right to our service.

If we made so many bricks for Pharaoh, "What shall we render unto the Lord." If fear produced activity, how much more should love?

4. Wings for Faith and Hope

Remember that God, who could deliver from Egypt, can and will bring us to Canaan.

Surely He who has commenced our deliverance will complete it.

5. A Call to Humility

I was but a servant, a slave. I owe all to my Deliverer. Without Him I would be a slave again. "By grace I am what I am."

Stems and Twigs

THE EVERLASTING ARMS

... underneath are the everlasting arms ... (Deut. 33:27).

1. The Arms of Everlasting Power (Jer. 31:17; 27:5; Luke 1:51)
2. The Arms of Everlasting Salvation (Isa. 45:17; 52:10; John 10:28; 1 Peter 1:5)
3. The Arms of Everlasting Redemption (Ps. 77:15; Ex. 6:6; Acts 13:17)
4. The Arms of Everlasting Protection (Ex. 15:16; Pss. 34:7; 91:16; John 10:28–29)
5. The Arms of Everlasting Sovereignty (Ezek. 20:33; Isa. 40:10; Pss. 97:1; 99:1; Rev. 19:6).
6. The Arms of Everlasting Judgment (Isa. 51:5; Jer. 21:5; John 5:22)
7. The Arms of Everlasting Victory (Ps. 98:1; 1 Cor. 15:57; 1 John 5:4)

Treasures of Bible Truth, William H. Schweinfurth

Everlasting Perfume

Perfumers are constantly striving to develop a permanent fragrance. Jasmine is the most lasting. Ahmed Soliman of Cairo, Egypt, declares that to make one ounce of jasmine he fills a room with unblemished blossoms, and that when they are distilled, the fragrance is almost everlasting. At Luxom, an archeologist found an ancient tomb in which a princess had been buried five thousand years before. In the tomb a vase had been filled with perfume that she might enjoy its jasmine fragrance through the ages. The scent was still there, though the vase was broken. Yet, enduring as jasmine may be, there is no perfume that is able to outlast that which comes from the Rose of Sharon, the Lord Jesus, dwelling in the human heart!

Selected

SAINTS IN GOD'S HAND

. . . all his saints are in thy hand (Deut. 33:3).

I. **Who Are Saints?** They are children of God by regeneration. They are "born of the Spirit," "born again," "new creatures," "created in Christ Jesus unto good works."

II. **Saints Are in God's Hand.** It may be said that all God's creatures are in His hand; but the saints are so in a peculiar sense. This will appear if we consider—

A. *They are in His loving hand.* His is the hand of a Father and surely He loves those whom He has made His children in so costly a manner, even through the incarnation and death of His own Son.

B. *They are in His guiding hand.* Well it is for them that they are not left to their own guidance. They know not the way in which they should go. They know not what is best for them.

C. *They are in His protecting hand.* How greatly they need protection! They need protection from themselves, protection from the evil influences of the world and from the snares of Satan. His hand is stretched forth for their defense.

D. *They are in His chastening hand.* He chastens them with the paternal reluctance exemplified in a wise earthly father (Lam. 3:33). His love prompts the application of the chastening rod (Heb. 12:5–11).

E. *They are in His sustaining hand.* He upholds them. Otherwise they would sink beneath the waves of sorrow. The hour of death approaches. How greatly will they need divine support in that hour when all human helpers fall!

Notes of Sermons

A poor, unlettered, old woman was once asked by a skeptic, "Well, Betty, so you are one of the saints, are you? Pray, what sort of folks are they? What do you know about religion?"

"Well, well," replied the old woman, "you know, sire, I'm no scholar, so I can't say much for the meaning of it. I only know I'm 'saved by grace,' and that's enough to make me happy here, and I expect to go to heaven by and by."

"Oh, that's all, is it? But surely you can tell us something nearer than that. What does being saved feel like?"

"Why, it feels to me," said the Spirit-taught one, "just as if the Lord stood in my shoes, and I stood in His." *Gospel Light*

SEVEN-FOLD PRIVILEGE OF THE CHILD OF GOD

Deut. 33:3–29

Saved .... Deuteronomy 33:29

Secured .... Deuteronomy 33:3

Separated .... Deuteronomy 33:16

Satisfied .... Deuteronomy 33:23

Sheltered .... Deuteronomy 33:29

Seated .... Deuteronomy 33:3

Sacrificing .... Deuteronomy 33:19

Pegs for Preachers

THE HAPPY PEOPLE

The eternal God is thy refuge, and underneath are the everlasting arms: and he shall thrust out the enemy from before thee; and shall say, Destroy them . . . (Deut. 33:27–29).

I. The People Described
   A. A *saved* people
   B. A *happy* people
   C. A *victorious* people

II. The Nature of Their Blessedness
   A. Their *shelter*
   B. Their *support*
   C. Their *security*
   D. Their *provisions*
   E. Their *defense*
   F. Their *assurance* of victory

Pulpit Germs

LOVE FOR THE HOUSE OF GOD

Lord, I have loved the habitation of thy house, and the place where thine honor dwelleth (Ps. 26:8).

I. God's House in Its Relation to the Devout Worshiper

A. As the appointed place for divine worship.

We are not indifferent to the truth that there is no spot on earth where the throne of grace is not accessible. Yet the sacred sanctuary, set apart for God's special worship and hallowed by the prayers of many of His people, claims to be regarded with special love and reverence, whether it be tabernacle or temple, church or chapel.

B. As the place where God has especially promised to reveal Himself to His people.

God allowed a visible emblem of His Presence to dwell in the tabernacle of old and in His house today. He is especially present to convict, to comfort, and to bless.

C. God's house is loved by the Christian because of hallowed experience there.

Its services develop and sanctify the social bond in all its relations. It is loved as the type of the house not made with hands, eternal in the heavens.

II. Some of the Tokens of True Regard and Love for God's House

A. A desire to attend it.

B. A willingness to support it, both by taking part in its services and by loyally and generously giving of our substance for its maintenance.

C. By consistency of life, lest outsiders be offended by our actions, because of the sad difference between the prayers and practices of Christians.

Sermons in a Nutshell

A CALL TO WORSHIP

*O magnify the L*ORD *with me, and let us exalt his name together (Ps. 34:3).*

This text is a clear call to sincere worship. To respond to the call will enable souls to have strength to meet the onslaughts of life. Among the lessons in the text are:

1. The Purpose of Worship Is Stated

"O magnify the Lord." The primary purpose of worship is to magnify the Lord and to exalt His holy name that we may receive strength in so doing. The Lord is worthy of worship. His character is good, His deeds are merciful, His acts are just, and His love is everlasting. Reverence the Lord! Adore Him! Magnify His works! Exalt His holy name!

2. The People for Worship Are Mentioned

"With me." The psalmist expresses his praise to the Father and then calls for all people everywhere to join him in holy worship. Truly all people should worship the Lord for His goodness. In other places in the Psalms the writer calls on all things to praise the Lord, even the heavens to be glad, the earth to rejoice, the fields to be happy, and the trees to sing for joy. Surely all people should pray and worship God. All need to worship Him. All would be blessed in worship.

3. The Place of Worship Is Intimated

"Let us exalt his name together." This calls for the unity of an assembly. It calls for people to assemble themselves together and worship the Lord in the unity of purpose. It is a glorious truth that men may worship the Lord in any and all places. But it is true also that there is an inspiration in a congregation worshiping the Lord together in the beauty of holiness. It is glorious that the people of our nation are within easy reach of a place erected and dedicated unto the Lord for worship.

4. The Plan of Worship Is Suggested

"His praise shall continually be in my mouth." Many may praise the Lord in song and prayer and testimony and witnessing. These methods may be used in private and in public as people seek to worship and magnify the Lord and His blessed name and work.

"O magnify the Lord." Worship His holy name!

Author Unknown

TOGETHER

We took sweet counsel together, and walked unto the house of God in company (Ps. 55:14).

Togetherness (cooperation) should characterize:

1. Our Worship

Private worship and radio worship have their value but are no substitute for public worship. "Forsake not the assembling of yourselves together."

2. Our Financial Support of the Church

"On the first day of the week let every one of you lay by . . ." (1 Cor. 16:2).

3. Our Warfare for Christ

Christian soldiers must not be divided, or scattered.

Snappy Sermon Starters

FOLLOW YOUR LEADER

And he led them on safely, so that they feared not (Ps. 78:53).

I. Led.

II. Led on.

III. Led on Safely.
   A. Hence they feared not.

IV. Who Is Our Leader?
   A. "I have given him for a leader" (Isa. 55:4).

V. Whom Does He Lead?
   A. The redeemed (Ex. 15:13).
   B. Those who know His mercy (Isa. 49:10).

VI. How Does He Lead?
   A. In the way we should go (Isa. 48:17).
   B. "In the paths of righteousness" (Ps. 23:3).

Hence there is no need to fear (see Isa. 41:10–13; Ps. 23:4; Heb. 13:5–6). *Snappy Sermon Starters*

THE ETERNAL CITY

Glorious things are spoken of thee, O city of God (Ps. 87:3).

1. **A Place of Supreme Happiness.**
   "Fullness of joy" (Ps. 16:11).
   "God shall wipe away all tears" (Rev. 7:17).

2. **A Place of Surpassing Beauty.**
   "Eye hath not seen nor ear heard" (1 Cor. 2:9).
   "The half has never been told."

3. **A Place of Revelation.**
   "Now we know in part, then . . ." (1 Cor. 13:12).

4. **A Place of Freedom from Pain.**
   "There shall be no more pain" (Rev. 21:4).
   Deaf . . . Blind . . . Lame . . . Healed (Isa. 35).

5. **A Place of Reunion.**
   "Then . . . face to face" (1 Cor. 13:12).
   "Many shall come from the east and west . . ." (Matt. 8:11).

Snappy Sermon Starters

THE PURPOSE OF PRAISE

Bless the Lord, O my soul, and forget not all his benefits (Ps. 103:2).

1. **It Is Praise to God**

   "Bless the Lord." The Lord gives life and sustains it. We live and move and have our life in Him. We should praise Him for every good and perfect gift. We should praise Him for all physical and spiritual blessings. The Lord is worthy of all praise from all the people in all the earth.

2. **It Is Praise from the Soul**

   "O my soul." The praise uttered here comes from a full heart. It is the very expression of the soul. The praise expressed here is from all the faculties and powers of the being. It expresses all that can come from the intellect, the feeling, and the will of a grateful personality. This praise is the voice of the sincere soul. Such praise will lift the soul into the very presence of God.

3. It Is Praise for Benefits

"Forget not all his benefits." Praise the Lord for all He does for us in the physical and the spiritual realms. Study the seven benefits of the Lord mentioned in Psalm 103:3–6. He forgives our sins and saves our souls, and we become children of His. He is the Great Physician and can heal all the diseases of the body when it is in accord with His holy will. He preserves life, crowns it with lovingkindness, supplies every good thing that life needs, and gives continually the strength we need. How gracious is the Lord! What benefits to have Him always! Praise Him! Bless His name!

Sermons in Outline, Jerome O. Williams

THE MERCHANT

The merchandise of it is better than the merchandise of silver, and the gain thereof than fine gold (Prov. 3:14).

This is one of the most forceful and impressive of all the proverbs of Solomon. He takes a merchant who traffics in silver and gold to set forth the reality and activities of religion. The holy experience of grace and Christ's righteousness in the soul is as much of a reality as silver and gold is real.

I. The Analogy.

A. The merchant wisely locates his business for success.
  1. So the Christian will first locate his gifts of prayer, song, strength, and whatever God has given him for service.
B. The wise merchant fills his place with goods for sale.
  1. The Christian for happiness and usefulness will see to it that his heart is filled with holy experience, grace, and truth.
C. The successful merchant advertises his business to the world.
  1. The Christian will likewise ever be ready to give his testimony to win souls.
D. The merchant has great concern about the prices of goods and general state of the market.

1. The child of God will in like manner have deep interest about the affairs and state of Zion.
E. The retail merchant keeps up a frequent correspondence with the great trading marts.
1. So with the faithful Christian.
2. He will be constant in prayer and have correspondence with the divine Lord.
F. Merchants differ in talents, some with large and some with smaller gifts.
1. So with Christians; but all are to give service to the best of their ability.
G. The successful merchant accommodates himself to his customers.
1. The faithful Christian will always be on the alert to suit his words, acts, and influence to the best good of those around him.
H. A good merchant both dispenses and receives benefits.
1. He sells for the benefit of others and receives profits himself.
2. So the useful Christian—he gives blessings to others and thereby receives benefit to his own soul.
I. The successful merchant closes up his life work with large gain.
1. How many earnest and faithful Christians will have their crowns bedecked with stars, and yet walk the golden streets with those they have led to Christ.

II. The Application.

Will everyone who hears this discourse enter at once into holy traffic for Jesus as you never have before?

Revival Sermons in Outline

SEVEN REASONS FOR STUDYING THE BIBLE

Thy word have I hid in mine heart, that I might not sin against thee (Ps. 119:11).

1. It Is Commanded
"Study to shew thyself approved unto God, a workman that needeth not to be ashamed, rightly dividing the word of truth" (2 Tim. 2:15).

2. It Reveals the Way of Salvation
"And that from a child thou hast known the holy scriptures, which are able to make thee wise unto salvation through faith which is in Christ Jesus" (2 Tim. 3:15; 1 Cor. 15:1–4; Rom. 1:16).

3. It Gives Assurance to the Believer
"My sheep hear my voice, and I know them, and they follow me: and I give unto them eternal life; and they shall never perish, neither shall any man pluck them out of my hand" (John 10:27–28; Phil. 1:6).

4. It Is Profitable
"All scripture is given by inspiration of God, and is profitable for doctrine, for reproof, for correction, for instruction in righteousness: that the man of God may be perfect, thoroughly furnished unto all good works" (2 Tim. 3:16; 1 Tim. 4:8).

5. It Will Endure Forever
"But the word of the Lord endureth forever. And this is the word which by the gospel is preached unto you" (1 Peter 1:25).

"Heaven and earth shall pass away: but my words shall not pass away" (Mark 13:31; Ps. 119:89).

6. It Will Give Great Peace
"Great peace have they which love thy law: and nothing shall offend them" (Ps. 119:165).

7. It Will Judge in the Last Day
"He that rejecteth me, and receiveth not my words, hath one that judgeth him: the word that I have spoken, the same shall judge him in the last day" (John 12:48).

William Schweinfurth

THE PRAYERS TO WHICH GOD LISTENS

Proverbs 15:29

1. **God does not listen to the prayers of:**
   —Those who "regard iniquity in their hearts" (Ps. 66:18).
   —The haughty and self-sufficient (Luke 18:11).
   —The uncharitable (Prov. 21:13).
   —Those who need not God's Word (Prov. 28:9).
   —Selfish people (James 4:3).

2. **God does listen to the prayers of:**
   —The humble (Luke 18:13–14).
   —The righteous (James 5:16).
   —Those who abide in Him (John 15:7).
   —The destitute (Ps. 102:17).
   —The afflicted (James 5:13).
   —Seekers of wisdom (James 1:5).

Paul E. Holdcraft

OUR WONDERFUL SAVIOR

. . . his name shall be called Wonderful . . . (Isa. 9:6).

W—Wonderful in His Work .... (John 7:21; 9:4; 17:4)

O—Wonderful in His Offering .... (Heb. 10:10, 14, 18)

N—Wonderful in His Nature .... (Col. 2:9; John 10:30; 14:9)

D—Wonderful in His Deeds .... (John 5:19; Mark 7:37)

E—Wonderful in His Example .... (1 Peter 2:21)

R—Wonderful in His Redemption .... (Col. 1:14; Eph. 1:7; 1 Peter 1:18–20)

F—Wonderful in His Forbearance .... (Mark 15:3–5)

U—Wonderful in His Union .... (John 17:21–23)

L—Wonderful in His Love .... (John 15:13; 13:1)

Treasures of Bible Truth

THE THREEFOLD WORK OF THE HOLY SPIRIT

John 16:7–11

1. To Convict of Sin
2. To Convince of Righteousness
3. To Warn of Judgment to Come

Author Unknown

WHAT DANIEL WAS

Daniel 6

1. **A Praying Man.**
   "He kneeled and prayed" (6:10).
2. **A Praising Man.**
   "And gave thanks" (6:10).
3. **A Persecuted Man.**
   "Cast him into the den of lions" (6:16).
4. **A Protected Man.**
   "Hath shut the lions' mouths" (6:22).
5. **A Persistent Man.**
   "Thou servest continually" (6:20).
6. **A Privileged Man.**
   "God, whom thou servest" (6:20).
7. **A Prosperous Man.**
   "So this Daniel prospered" (6:28).
8. **A Preferred Man.**
   "This Daniel was preferred" (6:3).

Author Unknown

THE BEST PROTECTION

Thou wilt keep him in perfect peace, whose mind is stayed on thee: because he trusteth in thee (Isa. 26:3).

1. **The Recipient of the Promise**—The man "whose mind is stayed."

   "Mind," in margin "thought," includes imagination, idea, desire, whole heart. "Stayed"; by deliberate act of faith shifting all care, responsibility, result, to the One best able to take it; and being, in consequence, left at peace from all worry.

2. **The Precious Assurance Here Given**—"Thou wilt keep him in perfect peace."

   Peace is longed for by all: individuals and nations. It is God's gift, bestowed only on those who fulfill His conditions.

   Peace, God-given, is peace at its fullest. "Perfect peace," in the original "Peace, peace," language failing to express its fullness—like *ff* or *pp* in music, for much loudness or much softness.

3. **The Simple, Yet Ample Reason Assigned**—"Because he trusteth in Thee."

   It is the direct outcome of faith. So simple that none can fail to find it. "He trusteth in Thee"; ample ground for faith, for Jehovah is the Covenant God.

The "trust" of the Old Testament is just the "faith" of the New. Let us, therefore, who have come to God through Christ, allow the peace of God to rule in our hearts. So shall we have peace indeed in our hearts and homes—peace in the present, and peace for the future. *Sermons in a Nutshell*

The story is told of the famous scientist, Albert Einstein, who forgot his spectacles in the Pullman when he went to the diner to eat. He picked up the menu and tried to read it without success. The waiter approached for his order. Einstein handed the menu card to him with the request that he read it for him. The waiter fumbled a second with the card and then confessed:

"I can't see it either."

Faith is like a pair of spectacles. No matter how famous or brilliant one may be, it is only by means of faith that one is able to apprehend the things of God. *J. B. Tweter*

WITH WINGS AS EAGLES

They that wait upon the LORD shall renew their strength; they shall mount up with wings as eagles (Isa. 40:31).

Many metaphors and similes are used in Scripture to help the people of God to understand themselves: sheep, salt, light, branches, soldiers, leaven, etc.

In the text the man of God is compared to the greatest of the fowls of the air, the eagle.

I. The Eagle Is Noted for Great Strength.
   A. Christians should be "strong in the Lord," etc.
   B. Christians should never be "weary in welldoing."

II. The Eagle Is Noted for Its Farsightedness.
   A. "The Christian on his knees sees more than the philosopher on tiptoes."
   B. Stephen's "eagle eyes"—vision of Son of God.
   C. Daniel's window open toward Jerusalem.

III. The Eagle Rises Above the World, Which Is Enveloped By Gases, Smoke, Dust, and Clouds.
   A. The Christian rises above the sordid things of the world.
   B. The Christian walks on the earth, but his head is above the clouds.
   C. Man's soul longs for freedom from sin.

IV. The Eagle Is Noted for Longevity.
   A. The Christian will live forever.

Snappy Sermon Starters, Paul E. Holdcraft

A man, not long converted, attended a Christian convention for the first time. After the first session, the friend who had brought him to the convention said, "Well now, did you enjoy the first part of our convention?" The new convert hesitated, then replied, "To be honest, if I had still been unsaved and you had brought me here, I would have thought to myself: How defeated this group of people look! There's something wrong, isn't there?" When the other man agreed, the new convert said, "Please don't think I want to find fault, but 'droopy' Christians always puzzle me, and they do a great deal of harm. I'm only a new Christian, but by God's grace I want to show forth the victory that is in Christ for us. Isn't that what is meant by the power of His resurrection?"   *From a radio sermon*

THE ANTIDOTE TO FEAR

Fear thou not; for I am with thee ... (Isa. 41:10).

Fear is common to man, increased by, if it does not originate in, a consciousness of sin. The text indicates three reasons why the Christian should not be afraid.

I. God's Presence
"I am with thee."
Powerful, wise, loving.

II. God's Relationship
"I am *thy* God."

These words imply on our part reverence, obedience, and submission; on His part guardianship and blessing. We naturally take special care of that which is our own.

III. God's Promise
    A. "I will strengthen thee"—fortify thy heart against trial and suffering.
    B. "I will help thee"—render thee personal assistance; direct, protect, fight with and for thee.
    C. "I will uphold thee."
        "The right hand of My righteousness." My faithful right hand: i.e., a hand that could be relied upon.
        1. The right hand is generally used for work.
        2. The right hand is offered in friendship.
        3. The right hand is placed on those whom we wish to honor.

The Preacher's Treasury

Overheard in an Orchard

Said the Robin to the Sparrow:
    "I should really like to know
Why these anxious human beings
    Rush about and worry so."

Said the Sparrow to the Robin:
    "Friend, I think that it must be
That they have no heavenly Father
    Such as cares for you and me."

Elizabeth Cheney

WITNESSES

Ye are my witnesses (Isa. 43:10).

I. Why Has God Chosen the Believer for This Work?

A. Because he knows experimentally more of God than any other being. Angels could witness of His majesty and goodness. Devils, of His wrath and justice. All men, of His wisdom. But a child of God, while witnessing to all these, can tell of His mercy, of His forgiving love, of His forbearance, tenderness, and loving-kindness.

B. Because he can have no greater joy. The bride's delight is to point out her Lord, saying, "This is my friend; this is my beloved." It is by grace we are permitted to testify of Christ.

C. Because of our being constantly in the presence of our fellowmen. He would have the world without excuse. For from her very midst He raises up His witnesses.

II. The Things a Believer Must Possess in Order to Witness for Christ.

A. *Knowledge.* He must know by experience the truth of God's Word. His life must be one "amen" to the words of his Lord. Thus, the Master says, "My yoke is easy," "Him that cometh"—the witness says, It is so; His yoke is easy; He has received and saved *me*.

B. *Veracity.* However distasteful to men, we must speak the truth. The martyrs died amid flames because they would speak the truth as they themselves apprehended it.

C. *Consistency.* Can one who says "this" today and "that" tomorrow, be believed? If you are most sanctimonious on Sunday and most worldly all the week, who will value your testimony?

D. *Patience.* In our courts of law a witness has often a long wait. And though he attests the uprightness of a beggar, he waits. Remember, we witness of the Judge!

E. *Boldness, firmness.* The world will do its cross-examining trying to catch us in our speech, as it did Christ.

III. The Best Methods Christ's Witness Can Adopt.

What are they? A parade of private devotion? Learned expositions of your creed? Denunciation of your opponents? Seclusion in a hermit's cell? No, but rather—

A. A daily manifestation of heart-loyalty to Christ.

B. A daily feeding on His promises, thus showing contentment and hope.

C. A growing in His likeness.

D. The display of the graces of His Spirit.

Stems and Twigs

THE DESIRE OF ALL NATIONS

And the desire of all nations shall come: and I will fill this house with glory, saith the Lord of hosts (Hag. 2:7).

I. Jesus Was the Desire of All Nations:

A. As the Kinsman of the whole family.

B. Because He only could bestow those precious blessings which the world needed.

C. Because all nations shall one day be made happy in Him.

II. He Appeared:

A. At the very period marked out for His birth.

B. In the very manner which had been foretold.

C. For the performance of the very work which had been before marked out for Him.

III. The Prophet Haggai Mentions Certain Remarkable Events Which Should Distinguish the Messiah's Coming:

A. All nations were to be shaken.

B. The Jewish temple should be filled with His glory.

Snappy Sermon Starters

SPIRITUAL WORSHIP

But the hour cometh, and now is, when the true worshipers shall worship the Father in spirit and in truth: for the Father seeketh such to worship him (John 4:23).

I. **We Must Worship God in His True Nature.**
   A. Personality
   B. Unity

II. **We Must Worship Him in the Right Relation.**
   A. Our Father
   B. Reconciled

III. **We Must Worship Him in the Right Manner.**
   A. In spirit—opposed to place, ceremonies, formality
   B. In truth—through the medium of Christ the Truth

Pulpit Germs

New Testament

THE NAME OF JESUS

Thou shalt call his name Jesus: for he shall save his people from their sins (Matt. 1:21).

Almost every historic person in the Bible bears an appropriate name; thus the name came to be identified with the person. In this text the name Jesus is declared to be descriptive of the person and the work of Christ.

I. Let Me Call Your Attention to the Savior.

Jesus signifies: "Jehovah that saves." So Jesus is divine: He saves His people from their sins. Not the word, not the ordinances, but Jesus Himself.

II. Look at the Salvation.

A. Jesus saves from sin by bestowing forgiveness—full forgiveness, free, immediate, and irreversible.

B. Jesus saves His people from the pollution of sin; not in their sins, but from their sins. It is true that holiness is progressive, but the Christian cannot and does not love sin. Nor can he live in sin as the choice and habit of his life. This salvation shall be completed in heaven.

III. Let Us Look at the Saved.

"He shall save His people."

A. Who are His people?

They must have been at one time in their sins. Therefore no one need despair.

"But does not the phrase speak of election? And how do I know that I am elected?"

Your business is not with election but with your calling, and you may make your calling sure by believing. Whosoever believeth in Him shall not perish. "Whosoever." Everyone feels that includes him. "Whosoever believeth." Does that include you?

Three Hundred Outlines on the New Testament

THE CHRISTIAN'S LIGHT

Let your light so shine before men, that they may see your good works, and glorify your father which is in heaven (Matt. 5:16).

Christ, the Light of the world, says to His followers, "Ye are the light of the world." There is no real discrepancy between the two statements: the city is lit by lamps and yet it is the electricity that does it all.

I. **There Is First the Positive Injunction That Christians Are to Do Everything in Their Power to Secure That Their Light Shall Shine as Brightly as Possible.**
   This is to be done
   A. By the position we take up.
      1. A lamp on the floor will not send out its rays so widely as if it were suspended from the ceiling.
      2. The Christian should connect himself with the church, let his light shine by joining the company of those who confess with their mouths the Lord Jesus.
   B. By the character which we form.
      1. Character is the most important thing in the world.
      2. There is no eloquence so powerful as a good man's life.
   C. By the exertions we make for the conversion of fellow men.
      1. By these we benefit ourselves; let a man tie up his hand so that it becomes motionless, and by and by it will become withered and powerless.

II. **Look at the Negative Side of This Injunction.**
   A. We should remove everything that tends either to obscure or to hide our light, or which so affects it as to make it suggestive of ourselves rather than of God.
      1. We should get rid of the undue reserve by which multitudes are characterized.
      2. We must keep ourselves clear from all practical inconsistencies.
      3. We should avoid all self display. The best style in writing is that which gives the thought with such

transparency that the reader sees nothing else; and that is the noblest Christian character which shows the most of Christ.

Three Hundred Outlines on the New Testament

THE DUTY OF DISCIPLES

Seek ye first the kingdom of God, and his righteousness (Matt. 6:33).

It should be the supreme purpose of everyone to seek the kingdom of God. We study the text through five questions:

1. What Is to Be Done?
"Seek." Put your heart into this enterprise. Seek earnestly, diligently, enthusiastically, steadily, with your whole life, hands, head, and heart.

2. Who Is to Seek?
"Ye." All who believe in the Lord Jesus Christ. All who name the Name of Christ. All who are members of His Church and all who have a desire to do His will and follow His way. All who have had an experience of grace and possess a new heart, a new purpose, a new hope, a new outlook, and a new Master. "Seek ye."

3. When Shall We Seek?
"First." In time. In aim. In activity.

4. What Shall We Seek?
His kingdom and His righteousness. Seek to be right in every relation of life, in relation to God, to Christ, to the church, to all Christians, to all sinners.

5. Why Should We Seek?
Because when we attain righteousness and seek the kingdom, all lesser blessings will be added unto us. When we seek the kingdom and righteousness of the Lord, He will see that we have all necessary food and clothing and raiment. It is a promise of the Lord.

Sermons in Outline

CONFESSING CHRIST

Matthew 10:32

The text is greatly emphasized by the circumstances of its utterance.

I. The Object to Be Confessed.
A. Not our good works, church membership, or worthy desires and purposes.
B. Not some remarkable experience.
C. But Christ as our Savior and King, our trust in Him for pardon, and our obedience to Him as our Lawgiver.

II. To Whom the Confession Is to Be Made.
A. To Christ—the heart.
B. To men—"before men" (Rom. 10:9–10). Do not hesitate from any cause. Remember:
    1. Christ requires it.
    2. He knows all about you.
    3. He wants to use your confession.

III. The Manner of Confessing.
A. By words; "with the mouth confession is made unto salvation."
B. By acts; the ordinances and an upright life.

IV. The Promise to Those Confessing.
They shall be confessed before the Father.
A. Confessed now, which means forgiveness, reconciliation and unspeakably rich blessings in the life that now is.
B. Confessed hereafter; received into glory; welcomed by the King in His beauty; "Come ye blessed of my Father."

V. How Simple the Requirement, How Wonderful the Reward!

Revival Sermons in Outline

THE EASY YOKE AND THE LIGHT BURDEN

For my yoke is easy, and my burden is light (Matt. 11:30).

I. **The Yoke of Christ Is Easy**, and His burden is light, because we bear it with the approbation of conscience. A burden which does not consist of sin is never heavy.

II. **This Yoke Is Easy** because it is borne in love.

III. **Christ's Yoke Is Easy** and His burden is light because it is borne with the help of the Spirit of God.

IV. **Christ's Words Are True** because His burden becomes lighter the longer it is borne.

V. **Christ's Yoke Is Easy** and His burden light because we are sustained under it by a good hope.
   A. Heaven and endless happiness are reserved for us.

Three Hundred Outlines on the New Testament

THE BELIEVER'S POSITION

Given out of the world .... (John 17:6)

Sent into the world .... (John 17:18)

Left in the world .... (John 17:11)

Not of the world .... (John 17:14)

Hated by the world .... (John 17:14)

Kept from the evil of the world (John 17:15)

Pegs for Preachers

THE PRESENCE OF JESUS

... Jesus went unto them, walking on the sea ... (Matt. 14:25–33).

1. The Problem of His Presence
"They were troubled." "They cried out for fear." They did not recognize Jesus. He is always present. He is with us always. We should always be able to recognize Him and be willing to honor Him everywhere.

2. The Proof of His Presence
Jesus assured the disciples of His presence with the same clear voice that they had often heard. He said, "Be of good cheer; it is I; be not afraid." Hear the voice of Jesus who comes to us just when we need Him most.

3. The Permission of His Presence
There was doubt in the heart of Peter, and Jesus gave him permission to walk on the water and to come to Him, but Peter's faith failed when he took his eyes off Jesus and saw the boisterous waves. Jesus is willing to be tried.

4. The Power of His Presence
When Peter began to sink, he cried unto Jesus, "Lord, save me." Jesus stretched forth His hand and lifted the disciple out of trouble and calmed the waves. Jesus has power to control nature. He has all power and will manifest it to save the people. Call on Him.

5. The Praise of His Presence
"They that were in the ship came and worshiped him, saying, 'Of a truth thou art the Son of God.'" Hearts of praise should be lifted to Jesus for all that He is to our weak and failing lives. Praise Him. Worship Him. Love Him. Live in the presence of Jesus and allow Him to give blessings.

Sermons in Outline

GREAT FAITH

O woman, great is thy faith: be it unto thee even as thou wilt (Matt. 15:28).

"Faith is the substance of things hoped for, the evidence of things not seen."

1. "Great Faith" Leads to Great Undertakings
It was a great undertaking for this woman to come to Christ.

2. "Great Faith" Begets Great Expectations
She expected the Savior to heal her daughter. We often expect no great results from our labors, because we do not have this great faith.

3. "Great Faith" Awakens Great Earnestness
She cried and fell at His feet and worshiped Him. Look at the earnestness of Knox, Luther, Wesley, etc. They had great faith.

4. "Great Faith" Conquers Great Difficulties
First it is said, "He answered her not a word." But she kept on. Next He said He was not sent but to the lost sheep of the house of Israel. Still she is not discouraged. Next He said, "It was not meet to take the children's bread and cast it to the dogs." She answered, "Truth, O Lord," etc. What difficulties have not been overcome by those of undaunted courage and faith!

5. "Great Faith" Achieves Great Victories
"Be it unto thee even as thou wilt" and her daughter was made whole (Mark 9:23; Matt. 17:20; Heb. 11:30–40).

100 Sermon Outlines

O for a Faith That Will Not Shrink

O for a faith that will not shrink,
    Though pressed by every foe,
That will not tremble on the brink
    Of any earthly woe!

That will not murmur nor complain
    Beneath the chastening rod,
But, in the hour of grief or pain,
    Will lean upon its God;

A faith that shines more bright and clear
    When tempests rage without;
That when in danger knows no fear,
    In darkness feels no doubt.

William H. Bathurst